FRANKLIN D. ROOSEVELT

PIVOTAL PRESIDENTS
PROFILES IN LEADERSHIP

FRANKLIN D. ROOSEVELT

Edited by Lorena Huddle

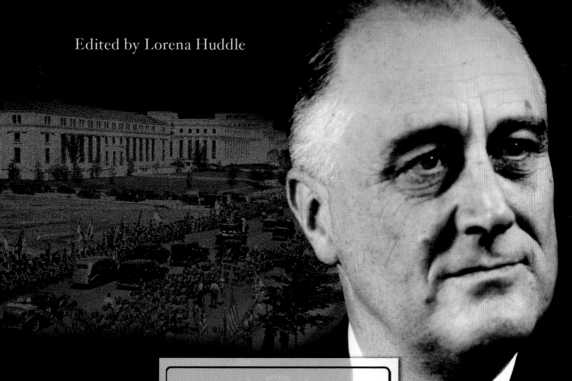

Britannica
Educational Publishing
IN ASSOCIATION WITH

ROSEN
EDUCATIONAL SERVICES

Published in 2017 by Britannica Educational Publishing (a trademark of Encyclopædia Britannica, Inc.) in association with The Rosen Publishing Group, Inc.
29 East 21st Street, New York, NY 10010

First Edition

Britannica Educational Publishing
J.E. Luebering: Executive Director, Core Editorial
Anthony L. Green: Editor, Compton's by Britannica

Rosen Publishing
Kathy Kuhtz Campbell: Senior Editor
Nelson Sá: Art Director
Ellina Litmanovich: Designer
Cindy Reiman: Photography Manager
Supplementary material by Lorena Huddle

Library of Congress Cataloging-in-Publication Data
Names: Huddle, Lorena, editor.
Title: Franklin D. Roosevelt / edited by Lorena Huddle.
Description: New York : Britannica Educational Publishing, 2017. | Series:
  Pivotal presidents: profiles in leadership | Includes bibliographical
  references and index. | Audience: Grade 7 to 12._
Identifiers: LCCN 2015050350 | ISBN 9781680485257 (library bound : alk. paper)
Subjects: LCSH: Roosevelt, Franklin D. (Franklin Delano), 1882-1945. |
  Presidents--United States--Biography. | United States--Politics and
  government--1933-1945.
Classification: LCC E807 .F687 2016 | DDC 973.917092--dc23
LC record available at http://lccn.loc.gov/2015050350

Manufactured in China

Table of Contents

During his presidency Franklin D. Roosevelt spoke directly to the American people in regular national radio broadcasts that became known as fireside chats.

Franklin D. Roosevelt was the only U.S. president elected to the office four times. In his 12 years in office, Roosevelt was both hated and loved. His opponents criticized him for the way he expanded the powers of the federal government. Most people, however, hailed him for his efforts to lead the United States through two of the greatest crises of the 20th century: the Great Depression and World War II.

Roosevelt started his career in politics in 1910, when he was elected as a Democrat to the New York Senate. In 1913 he was appointed assistant secretary of the Navy by President Woodrow Wilson. During World War I (1914–18) Roosevelt helped lead the Navy to victory over German sea forces. In 1920 he ran for vice president, but the Democrats lost the election.

In 1921 Roosevelt was stricken with poliomyelitis, a disease that paralyzed him from the waist down. In later years he could walk a little using a cane and leg braces, but he usually used a wheelchair (although not in public).

In 1928 and again in 1930 Roosevelt was elected governor of New York. During his governorship the worldwide economic downturn known as the Great Depression took hold. Roosevelt responded to the crisis by introducing programs to help the state's poor farmers and unemployed.

Roosevelt's aggressive relief policies in New York helped him to win the Democratic nomination for the presidency in 1932. In the election he won an easy victory over his Republican opponent, President Herbert Hoover, to become the 32nd president of the United States. By the time Roosevelt took office in 1933, the depression had deepened. Millions of Americans had no work and no money. The U.S. Congress granted Roosevelt unprecedented powers, and when it did not give him the powers he wanted, he simply assumed them. Roosevelt used his authority to create jobs and to help those who needed it. In doing so he changed the government's role in national life. For good or ill, many of Roosevelt's ideas of government are still part of the law of the land.

During World War II Roosevelt was the real commander in chief of the American armed forces in their successful effort to rid the world of German Nazism and Japanese militarism. He took charge of the industrial might of the United States and played a major part in setting up the United Nations.

In peace and in war Roosevelt always had the people behind him. Some of his methods may be questioned, but his aims were good. Readers of this book will learn about the character, intellect, and politics that shaped Roosevelt and made him the pivotal leader he came to be.

CHAPTER 1

Early Life, Education, and the New York Senate

F ranklin D. Roosevelt was born on January 30, 1882, at the family estate, Springwood, on the Hudson River near Hyde Park, New York. His father, James Roosevelt, was a wealthy landowner and railroad vice president. His mother was Sara Delano Roosevelt, of an old merchant-shipping family. She was James Roosevelt's second wife.

The birthplace and home of Franklin D. Roosevelt in Hyde Park, New York, became a "summer White House" while Roosevelt served as president.

Franklin was the only child of this second marriage. He had a half brother, 18 years older than he. President Theodore Roosevelt was their fifth cousin once removed. The Roosevelt family in America had been started by Klaes Martensen van Roosevelt. He came to America from Holland in about 1644.

Hyde Park, New York

Roosevelt's birthplace and home was the town of Hyde Park, in eastern New York. It lies on the east side of the Hudson River, 8 miles (13 kilometers) north of Poughkeepsie and about 75 miles (121 kilometers) north of New York City. The town (formed in 1821) bears the name of a local estate honoring Edward Hyde, Viscount Cornbury, who was governor of New York (1702–08).

President Roosevelt and his wife, Eleanor, are buried in Hyde Park at his family estate (290 acres [117 hectares]), which has been a national historic site since 1944. The adjacent Franklin D. Roosevelt Presidential Library and Museum contains some 44,000 books and houses Roosevelt's papers and memorabilia as well as a collection of material on U.S. and New York state history.

CHILDHOOD AND EDUCATION

Young Franklin was tutored at home until he was 14 years old. Nearly every year the family spent a few months in Europe. In the summers they vacationed at Campobello, a small Canadian island in the Bay of Fundy, near

Eleven-year-old Franklin sits for a portrait with his mother, Sara Delano Roosevelt.

Eastport, Maine. James Roosevelt took his son iceboating and tobogganing in the winter and fishing in the summer. He taught the boy about trees, horses, and dairy cattle, and how to run a farm.

As an only child, Franklin was given close attention, but he was not spoiled. His parents taught him standards of conduct that he was expected to follow without question. He rarely rebelled.

James Roosevelt's wealth allowed him to spend much time with his son. Franklin's mother, Sara Delano Roosevelt, was his real guide and teacher, however. She helped him with his schoolwork, watched his play, and saw that he ate well and slept soundly.

At age 10 Franklin began his lifelong interest in birds. He shot them and had them stuffed for his collection. While president he often went to the Hyde Park woods at dawn to watch birds and hear them sing.

About the same time he began another hobby that lasted nearly all his life—sailing. He sailed at Campobello and at home, first in his father's boats, then in his own. He started collecting ship models and books and pictures about the sea and ships. Still another interest was stamp collecting. At his death he had a huge and valuable collection.

In 1896 Franklin entered Groton School, a preparatory school in Groton, Massachusetts. The change from having his own tutor to being in classes with many other boys did not bother Franklin. He made friends at once and wrote enthusiastic letters home about school.

At Groton he received good grades and was active in several sports. In his last year he was manager of the baseball team. The school's headmaster, Endicott Peabody, an Episcopal clergyman, started the boy's thinking about public service.

After four years at Groton, he entered Harvard University. There he studied history, economics, languages, and science. His grades were good but not outstanding. All through college he was busy with extracurricular activities. He was especially interested in the *Crimson*, the student newspaper. He was the *Crimson* president and editor his last year.

His father died when Franklin was in college. Although his father left Franklin a good yearly income, Franklin was terribly saddened. His mother died in 1941, during his third term as president. In young adulthood Franklin was tall, well-built, slim, with light brown hair, blue eyes, and an engaging grin.

First Public Office

After graduation from Harvard Roosevelt attended Columbia University Law School in New York City. He completed his work in 1907 and began to practice with a leading New York law firm.

Meanwhile, on March 17, 1905, he married Anna Eleanor Roosevelt, his sixth cousin. President Theodore Roosevelt, Eleanor's uncle, came to New York City to give the bride away. The young couple saw much of "T. R." His liberal ideas and strong leadership helped Franklin decide on a career in public service.

In the next 10 years the Roosevelts had six children. The first was a daughter, Anna Eleanor, born 1906. The others were sons: James, born 1907; Elliott, born 1910; Franklin, Jr., born 1914; John, born 1916; and a son who died in infancy.

Roosevelt often visited Hyde Park and was active in community life. Democratic Party leaders saw that he would make a popular figure in politics. In 1910 they helped nominate him for state senator. The three counties that made up the Twenty-sixth District were solidly Republican in most years, but this time their voting strength was divided. Roosevelt

Eleanor Roosevelt was a niece of President Theodore Roosevelt. She married Franklin in New York City on March 17, 1905.

made a fighting campaign. Touring the district by car, he made dozens of speeches and impressed voters with his strong personality. He won by a narrow margin.

In Albany, the state capital, he made a good record. Brave and independent, he fought Tammany Hall, the New York City Democratic "machine." Tammany wanted to elect its man, William F. Sheehan, to the U.S. Senate. Roosevelt led the Democratic group that defeated Sheehan. He fought Tammany bills that benefited special groups. He worked for fuller regulation of public utilities, especially certain transportation lines.

In 1912 Roosevelt was reelected to the state senate, despite an attack of typhoid fever that kept him from making public appearances during the campaign. He worked for important bills to promote farm cooperation and to stop the unfair practices of commission (fruit and vegetable) merchants. He always regarded himself as an active farmer and liked to be called a country squire.

National Politics

I n 1911 it became clear that the long Republican control of national politics would be broken. The Republican Party was split when the new Progressive Party was formed. A Democratic victory was almost certain.

In 1912 Roosevelt strongly supported the nomination of Woodrow Wilson, a New Jersey Democrat, for president. He made speeches, wrote letters, and led 150 delegates to the Democratic convention in Baltimore. Party leaders liked his work. When the Wilson Administration came into office in March 1913, Roosevelt was offered several posts. He chose to become assistant secretary of the Navy, a post

Woodrow Wilson was elected the 28th president of the United States in 1912. Roosevelt served as Wilson's assistant secretary of the Navy from 1913 to 1920.

Theodore Roosevelt had held on his way to the presidency.

WAR SERVICE UNDER PRESIDENT WILSON

From 1913 to 1920 Roosevelt was a tireless assistant to Secretary of the Navy Josephus Daniels. In the years before the United States entered World War I, he worked for a larger and more efficient Navy. During

FDR as Assistant Secretary of the Navy

Roosevelt enthusiastically accepted the offer to become assistant secretary of the Navy. "All my life I have loved ships and have been a student of the Navy," he said. Roosevelt held the post from 1913 to 1920. He was a superb manager, and he got along well with sailors. During World War I he was responsible for obtaining and shipping supplies to the war front. One of Roosevelt's greatest feats during the war was persuading Great Britain to place mines in the North Sea to make it difficult for German submarines to navigate the area. Roosevelt also traveled to Europe to inspect naval bases and arrange naval contracts.

the war he helped lead the Navy to victory over German sea forces.

When the United States went to war in 1917, Roosevelt wanted to enter the armed forces. "Tell the young man," President Wilson said to Daniels, "his only and best war service is to stay where he is." Roosevelt stayed in Washington and worked hard. He was active in enlarging the Navy yards and improving their methods.

Additionally, Roosevelt built up the supply services. He supervised labor relations. He gave much time, thought, and energy to recruiting sailors. The Navy, which had about 75,000 men in peacetime, suddenly needed 500,000 men. The need was met, partly through Roosevelt's efforts.

DEFEATED FOR VICE PRESIDENT

In the 1920 presidential campaign, Roosevelt hoped to see his friend Governor Alfred E. Smith of New York nominated. He worked for Smith at the Democratic convention.

Instead, the nomination went to Governor James M. Cox of Ohio. Cox, from the Midwest, needed an Eastern vice presidential candidate as running mate. The delegates chose Roosevelt, whose war service, family name, and New York home made him a good political choice.

During the campaign Roosevelt made more than a thousand speeches. However, it was impossible to halt a war-weary

James M. Cox ran for the presidency as a Democrat in 1920 with Roosevelt as his running mate. He lost to the Republican candidate, Warren G. Harding.

nation's revolt against Democratic policies. The Republicans, Warren G. Harding and his running mate Calvin Coolidge, won by a landslide.

Polio and the Governorship

A fter the 1920 presidential election, Roosevelt returned to New York City. He became vice president of a financial firm, Fidelity and Deposit Company of Maryland. He also resumed his law practice.

POLIO STRIKES

Infantile paralysis, or poliomyelitis ("polio"), was widespread in the summer of 1921. In August, while on vacation at Campobello, Roosevelt was gripped by the disease. After days of pain and fever, he was left with the aftereffects of the disease—his legs were completely and permanently paralyzed. Yet polio did not stop him. Unable to take part in normal physical activities, he developed his mind further. As he made progress his belief in himself and his future grew. "Once I spent two years in bed trying to move my big toe," he said. "After that job, anything seems easy."

Careful exercise, plus winter treatments and swimming at Warm Springs, Georgia, brought back his strength. To benefit other polio sufferers, he helped to establish a treatment center at Warm Springs. In later years he could walk a little but only by using a cane, with his legs encased in steel braces, and usually with someone's help.

After Roosevelt was stricken with poliomyelitis, his wife, Eleanor, helped in his political career. Her own interest in politics increased during this time partly as a result of her desire to work for important causes.

NEW YORK GOVERNOR

Roosevelt founded the law firm of Roosevelt and Connor in 1924. The same year he went back to politics. At the Democratic convention he nominated Alfred E. Smith for president. Although Smith was not chosen this time, Roosevelt's "happy warrior" speech became famous. His contact with other political leaders throughout the country gave him a national following of devoted supporters.

Eleanor Roosevelt

A great reformer and humanitarian, Eleanor Roosevelt (1884–1962) strove to improve the lives of people all over the world. As the wife of Franklin D. Roosevelt, she had the distinction of being first lady longer than any other presidential wife—slightly more than 12 years (1933–45). Her defense of the rights of minorities, youths, women, and the poor during her tenure helped to shed light on groups that previously had been alienated from the political process.

After her husband's death in 1945, Eleanor made plans to retire, but she did not keep them. President Harry S. Truman appointed her a delegate to the United Nations, where she served as chairman of the Commission on Human Rights (1946–51) and played a major role in the drafting and adoption of the Universal Declaration of Human Rights. In 1961 President John F. Kennedy appointed her chairman of his Commission on the Status of Women, and she continued with that work until shortly before her death in 1962. She was buried at Hyde Park, her husband's family home on the Hudson River and the site of the Franklin D. Roosevelt Presidential Library and Museum.

By 1928 Smith had served four terms as governor of New York. At last he was chosen by the Democrats to run for president. Once more Roosevelt made the nominating speech. To strengthen the ticket in New York, the party asked Roosevelt to run for governor. In an exciting campaign he got both farm and city votes and won by a margin of 25,000. At the same time the Republican presidential candidate, Herbert Hoover, carried the state by 100,000 votes.

Smith had made New York one of the most progressive of all states. Roosevelt kept it in that position. His most notable fight was against the electric power interests. He accused them of trying to seize the St. Lawrence River waterpower on unfair terms. He stood for old-age pensions and unemployment insurance. Despite strong opposition he won an old-age security act that provided some benefits but not all he asked for. He obtained a law that limited the working hours of women and children. Poor farmers were given relief. Some farmers were transferred from poor lands to better homesteads, and waste areas were reforested.

In 1930 Roosevelt was reelected governor by a margin of 725,000 votes. The victory turned all eyes on him as a possible president. He continued his progressive course, hammering at better regulation of public utilities, court reform, and more attention to public health and housing. He favored organized labor and attacked prohibition of liquor. But he moved cautiously in dealing with New York City corruption. He removed a sheriff

People gather on the steps of the building across from the New York Stock Exchange on Black Thursday, October 24, 1929 — the start of the stock market crash in the United States.

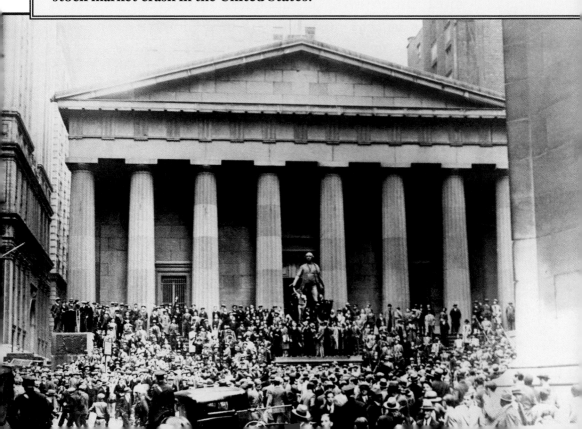

convicted of wrongdoing and helped to force the resignation of Mayor James J. Walker.

The stock-market crash of 1929 threw the nation's economic system into disorder. Within three years the national income was cut in half. By 1932 about 12 million Americans were out of work. Mortgages were foreclosed on thousands of homes and farms. Bank failures swept away savings. Factories shut down, mines closed, railroads went into bankruptcy. Many people searched for a new leader. Roosevelt's vigorous relief policies convinced them he was on their side.

CHAPTER 4

The Presidency and the Great Depression

The presidential campaign of 1932 was staged against the background of the Great Depression. Herbert Hoover, the Republican candidate for reelection, was almost sure to be defeated. Millions mistakenly blamed him for the depression. Some who wanted the Democratic nomination were Newton D. Baker of Ohio, John N. Garner of Texas, and Al Smith of New York.

A remarkable political manager, James A. Farley, set out to win delegates for Roosevelt across the country. He sent out booklets that told about Roosevelt's achievements in New York and that described his vote-getting strength. He wrote thousands of letters. He had Roosevelt telephone political leaders throughout the nation. Agents across the land wrote newspaper articles and talked to influential men. Long before the convention opened Roosevelt had a strong lead.

James A. Farley was an astute politician who organized Roosevelt's successful campaign for New York governor in 1928. He was also a key figure in Roosevelt's presidential campaign in 1932.

CAMPAIGN AND ELECTION

As the Democratic convention drew near, Roosevelt gathered a little group of experts, the "brain trust," who helped him shape his ideas. They backed his program of emphasizing economic problems. He made several good speeches outlining part of his plan for reviving the nation. In a speech in April 1932 he declared that the country faced a crisis more grave than in World War I. He said the country must build from the bottom up, not from the top down. He spoke of the "forgotten man at the bottom of the economic pyramid" as the man the government must help.

He called for a national program to help farmers, small banks, and homeowners. International trade was to be promoted by tariff reductions. Another speech called for bold experiments. With the nation in distress, it was common sense to try one plan, and if it failed, to try another.

The speeches impressed people. When the convention opened in Chicago, Roosevelt had a majority, but not two-thirds of the delegate votes required for nomination. There was danger that the other candidates would combine against him. At the critical moment Farley made an agreement by telephone with John N. Garner that released the Texas and California delegates to Roosevelt. On the fourth ballot,

---

A map shows the electoral results of the U.S. presidential election held on November 8, 1932. Roosevelt won with 472 electoral votes.

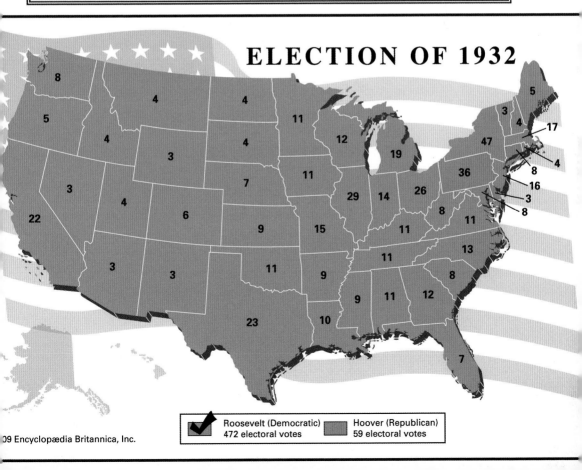

ELECTION OF 1932

8
5
4
22
3
4
4
3
3
3
6
4
7
9
11
23
4
4
11
11
10
15
9
12
19
29
14
11
9
11
26
8
11
12
36
8
13
8
47
3
4
5
17
8
4
16
3
8
11
7

☑ Roosevelt (Democratic)
472 electoral votes

Hoover (Republican)
59 electoral votes

09 Encyclopædia Britannica, Inc.

Roosevelt was nominated. Garner was chosen as the vice presidential candidate.

Roosevelt had already written his acceptance speech. He flew to Chicago and made his speech in person. This showed that he was prepared to act boldly and that polio would not hamper him as president. He said, "I pledge myself to a new deal. . . . This is more than a political campaign; it is a call to arms."

President Herbert Hoover fought a vigorous battle. He denounced Roosevelt's ideas as sure to endanger the American system. But the public was for Roosevelt. At the polls he carried all but six states. He

The First Inaugural Address

On March 4, 1933, the radio carried Roosevelt's voice throughout the nation. In his first inaugural address, he assessed the economic catastrophe of the Great Depression:

The withered leaves of industrial enterprise lie on every side; farmers find no markets for their produce;

the savings of many years in thousands of families are gone. More important, a host of unemployed citizens face the grim problem of existence, and an equally great number toil with little return. Only a foolish optimist can deny the dark realities of the moment.

But in the end, the address did much to restore public confidence. The speech is best remembered for these famous words of hope and courage:

This great Nation will endure as it has endured, will revive and will prosper. So, first of all, let me assert my firm belief that the only thing we have to fear is fear itself—nameless, unreasoning, unjustified terror which paralyzes needed efforts to convert retreat into advance.

had a popular plurality of some 7 million votes more than Hoover. Roosevelt's electoral vote was 472, and Hoover's was 59.

THE DEPRESSION DEEPENS

During the four months between Roosevelt's election and inauguration, he was very busy.

He was finishing his term as governor, planning his first steps as president, and selecting his Cabinet. He decided to call a special session of Congress to pass bills protecting farmers against mortgage foreclosures; relieving them through the domestic allotment plan; helping business by better bankruptcy procedures; and legalizing the sale of beer. He wanted to help Congress balance the budget. He also wanted to urge repeal of the 18th (Prohibition) Amendment.

In the winter of 1932–33 the depression deepened. Industrial production fell to the lowest level ever recorded. The nation seemed paralyzed. In city streets once-proud men sold apples or lined up for a free bowl of soup and a bed for the night. Yet the farms were full of food for which there was no market, and farmers formed into mobs to stop foreclosures. In factory towns few wheels moved, few chimneys smoked. Railroad trains ran empty. Banks failed by the hundreds. In January 1933 bank depositors became fearful and withdrew their savings in panic. The economic life of the nation was almost at a standstill.

President Hoover wanted Roosevelt to work with him on emergency measures.

Roosevelt's view was that without authority he could take no responsibility. He disagreed with Hoover on the causes of the depression. Hoover argued that national recovery had already begun but was being checked by disturbances and depression in Europe. Roosevelt held that home recovery had not yet started. The people lacked purchasing power, he said, and radical reforms were needed.

The New Deal

In his inaugural address Roosevelt had promised prompt, decisive action. He followed up on his promise by immediately launching the aggressive recovery program known as the New Deal. One goal of the program was to promote recovery. Another was to supply relief to the needy. A third goal was to furnish permanent reforms, especially in the management of banks and stock exchanges.

THE HUNDRED DAYS

A record number of bills were passed in the first three months of Roosevelt's presidency, which became known as the Hundred Days. Roosevelt's first step was to order all banks closed until Congress could address the banking crisis. Congress met in special session on March 9 and rushed through a bill that allowed only banks in sound condition to reopen. The "bank holiday," as Roosevelt called it, and the emergency legislation restored public confidence in banks. The administration then presented Congress with a broad array of additional measures to address the crisis.

A sign at a theater says that it would accept checks "drawn on local banks." Roosevelt had declared a "bank holiday" in March 1933, which closed all U.S. banks and permitted their reopening only after their solvency was verified by government inspectors.

THE AAA AND THE NRA

The most fought-over plans of the early New Deal were bills to raise the prices of farm and manufactured products while regulating farmers, manufacturers, and sellers. These measures made up a *planned economy*. They veered sharply from the old conservative ways of the American government. The Hoover Administration had set up the Reconstruction Finance Corporation to lend money to hard-pressed banks, railroads, and manufacturers. But Roosevelt's administration went much farther.

The first bill to pass was the Agricultural Adjustment Act (AAA). Its plan was to pay farmers for accepting government controls and was designed to cut down crop surpluses. Farmers growing wheat, corn, cotton, rice, and other staples for foreign trade were to place their farm operations under the secretary of agriculture. He was to reduce the acreage of overproduced staples and to divert part of the land to soil-improving crops or other uses. The president could inflate the currency by free coinage of silver, by printing more paper money, or by reducing the gold content of the dollar. Many Western farmers believed that this cheaper money would raise

Roosevelt signs the Agricultural Adjustment Act (AAA), a farm-relief bill, in 1933.

crop prices. The act also provided for federal loans to farmers at low interest rates.

The AAA was the most drastic law ever passed to help farmers. It controlled most of the 6 million American farms, whose owners had always been very independent. The law made cooperation voluntary. Farmers who disliked the plan might remain outside. However, most growers of export crops accepted it.

The National Industrial Recovery Act was an even more radical plan and affected a larger number of people. It set up a system of self-government by industry under federal supervision. For many years manufacturers had organized trade associations that drew up codes of fair trade practices and tried to enforce them. One object of these codes was to stop cutthroat competition. Many people believed that the depression was partly caused by such competition.

Roosevelt's team worked out a plan in which each branch of industry was to draft a fair business code. The codes were to be amended if necessary by the government. When accepted, they could be enforced in the federal courts. Labor was protected by code provisions abolishing child labor, setting maximum work hours and minimum pay rates, and arranging for collective bargaining. The National Recovery Administration (NRA) was set up to administer the law.

Many people regarded this legislation as a doubtful experiment. Trade associations with their codes could go a long way toward fixing prices. It was sometimes hard to tell their activities from those of the monopolies and trusts that the government had long attacked.

Fiorello La Guardia (*center*), the mayor of New York City, attends the formal raising of the National Recovery Administration (NRA) flag outside the New York headquarters of the NRA in April 1934.

For some months the country gave the NRA loyal support. Roosevelt was full of faith. He said history would probably declare it "the most important, far-reaching legislation ever enacted by an American Congress."

But as the codes became more complex and difficult to enforce, support for the NRA dwindled in the business community and in the government. In 1935 the Supreme Court declared the NRA to be unconstitutional.

THE TVA AND BANKING ACTS

Another spectacular reform measure was the Tennessee Valley Authority (TVA). During World War I a huge power dam to provide electric power for a nitrates plant was built at Muscle Shoals on the Tennessee River.

The Supreme Court of the United States, led by Chief Justice Charles Evans Hughes (*front center*), declared some of Roosevelt's New Deal measures unconstitutional, including the NRA and the AAA.

After that, public and private interests quarreled bitterly over the use of the Tennessee's waterpower. President Hoover favored private control. Senator George W. Norris of Nebraska fought for government ownership of hydroelectric plants on large rivers so that power could be sold cheaply. Now the new law set up a board to apply this idea to the Tennessee River.

Most bankers were convinced that banking abuses must be stopped. One abuse was the lending of huge sums for stock-market gambling. This helped to bring on the boom of 1928–29 and the crash that followed. The Glass-Steagall Banking Act gave the Federal Reserve Board control over interest rates and loans. Another abuse was the combining of commercial banks with investment banks. Many large commercial banks had investment branches that used depositors' money for speculating in securities. Now banks and investment houses were rigidly separated. The government also guaranteed bank deposits up to $5,000, so that small depositors would never again withdraw savings in a panic.

Millions of Americans had lost their savings in 1930–33 through frauds and misrepresentations in the sale of stocks and bonds. The Securities Act of 1933, which

Norris Dam, completed in 1936 and located northwest of Knoxville, was the first major Tennessee Valley Authority (TVA) construction project. It impounds the Clinch and Powell Rivers for hydroelectric power generation, flood control, and recreation.

The Tennessee Valley Authority

Until the 1930s the Tennessee River was virtually uncontrollable. In dry seasons it shrank to a mere trickle, and in time of heavy rainfall it flooded lowlands and washed away fertile soils. Croplands were continually eroded, and very little effort was made toward soil conservation. Although the Tennessee Valley was rich in natural resources, its inhabitants remained poor, and there was almost no industrial development.

To help lift the region out of poverty, the U.S. government established the Tennessee Valley Authority (TVA) as a public corporation in 1933. Its chief purpose was to harness the Tennessee River and its tributaries for flood control and navigation. A second purpose was to bring electrification to the area. Over the decades the TVA has done both, but the secondary purpose—electrification—soon assumed primary significance. In bringing electricity to the seven-state area it serves, the TVA is the largest public power producer in the United States.

was strengthened a year later, required that important facts on new securities be given to a federal agency and to all buyers.

Relief Measures

The Hundred Days also included relief measures, which provided jobs or short-term

New Civilian Conservation Corps (CCC) members wait to be fitted for shoes in 1935. CCC projects included planting trees, building flood barriers, and fighting forest fires.

payments to alleviate hardship. One bill set up the Civilian Conservation Corps (CCC). It gave 250,000 young men meals, housing, uniforms, and small wages for working in the national forests and other government properties. Another law set up the Federal Emergency Relief Administration (FERA), which made grants to the states for relief activities. The Public Works Administration (PWA) gave people work on roads, dams, public buildings, and other federal projects.

THE "SECOND NEW DEAL"

By 1934 the measures passed during the Hundred Days had produced some recovery. More important, they had inspired hope that the country would surmount the crisis. Yet Roosevelt knew he had to do more. Although the economy had begun to rise from its lowest point during the winter of 1932–33, it was still far below its level before the stock market crash of 1929. Millions of Americans were still unemployed, with many having been jobless for several years. Some people criticized the New Deal for not going far enough.

Roosevelt responded in 1935 by asking Congress to pass additional New Deal policies—sometimes called the Second New Deal. The key measures of the Second New Deal were the Social Security Act, the Works Progress Administration, and the Wagner Act.

Social Security Act

In his annual message to Congress in 1935, Roosevelt declared that the day of great private fortunes was ended. Instead, wealth must be better distributed. Every citizen must be

Roosevelt signs the Social Security Act into law on August 14, 1935.

guaranteed "a proper security, a reasonable leisure, and a decent living throughout life." It was time for the United States to follow Britain in providing insurance for unemployment and old age.

The Social Security Act was signed in August 1935. Under it the unemployed and the aged were to be looked after by combined state and federal action. To build up an unemployment insurance fund, a national tax, running to a high of 3 percent by 1939, was to be taken out of payrolls. The national government was also to help the states pay pensions to old people. A separate federal annuity system, based on wage earners' contributions, was to give every contributor a pension at age 65.

WORKS PROGRESS ADMINISTRATION

The Works Progress Administration (WPA) aimed to provide the unemployed with useful work that would help to maintain their skills and self-respect. The economy would in turn be stimulated by the increased purchasing power of the newly employed, whose wages under the program ranged from $15 to $90 per month.

During its eight-year existence, the WPA put some 8.5 million people to work (over 11 million were unemployed in 1934) at a cost to the federal government of approximately $11 billion. The agency's construction projects produced more than 650,000 miles (1,046,000 kilometers) of roads; 125,000 public buildings; 75,000 bridges; 8,000 parks; and 800 airports. The Federal Arts Project, Federal Writers' Project, and Federal Theater Project—all under WPA aegis— employed thousands of artists, writers, and actors in such cultural programs as the creation of art work for public buildings, the documentation of local life, and the organization of community theaters. Thousands of artists, architects, construction workers, and educators found work in American museums, which flourished during the Great Depression. The WPA also sponsored the National Youth Administration, which sought part-time jobs for young people.

WAGNER ACT

The Wagner Act of 1935—officially called the National Labor Relations Act—was the most important labor law passed in the United States in the 20th century. It established the legal right of most workers to organize or join labor unions and to bargain collectively with their employers. It also created the National Labor Relations Board (NLRB) to hear and resolve labor disputes.

REELECTION

In 1936 Roosevelt sought reelection with most big businessmen against him but with most farmers, workers, and small storekeepers on his side. His opponent, Alfred M. Landon of Kansas, was supported by about two-thirds of the nation's larger newspapers.

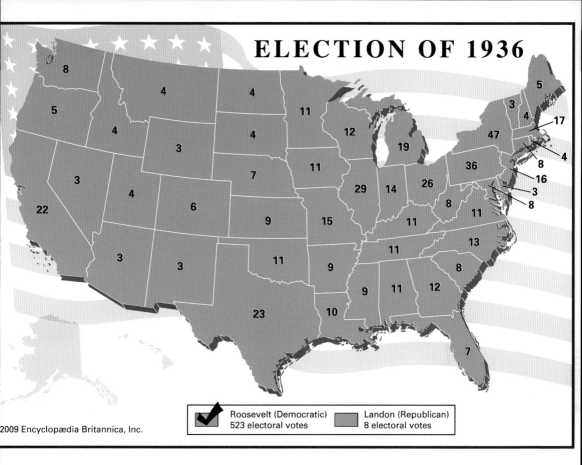

ELECTION OF 1936

8 · 4 · 4 · 11 · 5 · 3 · 4 · 17
5 · 4 · 4 · 12 · 19 · 47
3 · 3 · 36 · 8
3 · 4 · 7 · 11 · 29 · 14 · 26 · 16
22 · 6 · 9 · 15 · 11 · 8 · 3
3 · 3 · 11 · 9 · 11 · 11 · 13 · 8
9 · 11 · 12
23 · 10
7

| | Roosevelt (Democratic) 523 electoral votes | | Landon (Republican) 8 electoral votes |

2009 Encyclopædia Britannica, Inc.

A map displays the electoral results of the U.S. presidential election of 1936. Roosevelt received 523 electoral votes to Alfred M. Landon's 8.

Roosevelt's backers spent a little more than $5 million; Landon's backers spent about $9 million. Yet the result could be predicted long in advance. It was a Roosevelt landslide. The president carried 46 states, leaving Landon only Maine and Vermont. Roosevelt won by a plurality of 11,078,204 votes.

CHAPTER 6

Foreign Policy

I n foreign affairs Roosevelt was a follower of former president Woodrow Wilson. He wanted world peace, close friendship with Latin America and the British Empire, and more foreign trade. With Secretary of State Cordell Hull he pressed for tariff reductions. These were made possible by the Reciprocal Trade Agreements Act of 1934. This act allowed the president to make agreements to reduce tariffs mutually with other countries.

TRADE TREATIES — LATIN AMERICA

In his first inaugural address Roosevelt spoke of a "good neighbor" policy toward Latin

Cordell Hull served as Roosevelt's secretary of state from 1933 to 1944.

America. To carry it out, the United States gave up its old single-handed enforcement of the Monroe Doctrine. Instead it relied on enforcement by all American nations. It promised to no longer interfere in the internal politics of Latin American nations. In 1934 the United States gave up the Platt Amendment, under which it had the right to intervene in Cuba. The same year U.S. Marines left Haiti. Nor did the government stand behind

American investors in Latin American properties. In 1938 Mexico seized all the oil lands of American companies and failed to pay them adequately. The Roosevelt Administration made only mild and tactful protests.

Roosevelt tried hard to win Latin American confidence. The success of the Good Neighbor Policy was measured in part by the fact that most Latin American countries stood behind Roosevelt's policies as World War II drew near.

TROUBLE IN EAST ASIA

For years Roosevelt worked to awaken the United States to the dangers of war. He tried to halt the brutal acts of Japan, Italy, and Germany. He encouraged Britain, France, and other democracies.

Japan was the first to set the United States on guard. In 1931 it had overrun Manchuria. In 1932 it captured Shanghai and killed thousands of Chinese. President Hoover had refused to recognize Japan's puppet state of Manchukuo. He protested against Japan's efforts to block Chinese trade. When fighting began again in North China and at Shanghai and Nanking, Roosevelt was deeply troubled. At the same time Germans, Italians, and Soviets were fighting in the Spanish Civil War. Hitler and Mussolini were making warlike threats. Roosevelt spoke of a state of "international lawlessness."

Japan intended to conquer all China. American property and investments in China were worth $250 million. The United States valued Chinese trade. It had taken a special interest in Chinese education, missionary work, and democratic growth. In Chicago, on October 5, 1937, Roosevelt proposed that nations responsible for "international anarchy" should be quarantined. He said that the peace, freedom, and security of nine-tenths of the world were being threatened by the other tenth. The 90 percent that stood for peace and morality "can and must find some way to make their will prevail."

The response to this speech disappointed Roosevelt. Polls and newspapers showed that the nation did not want action. About two months later Japanese planes bombed and sank the American gunboat *Panay* and three American tankers. Japan apologized at once and the country remained calm.

American isolationism reached a high point in 1937–38. Congress passed a "permanent" neutrality law in 1937 to replace a temporary one passed two years earlier. It tried to guard the national peace and safety if a war broke out abroad. No loans, credits, or arms were to be given to either side. Even raw materials were not to be shipped except on a "cash and carry" basis and then only in foreign ships. Roosevelt and Hull objected to this law, for in a war of aggression America could not help the victim.

The best Roosevelt could do was to build up American defenses. Under his prodding Congress in May 1938 passed a billion-dollar appropriation. This was to build a Navy strong enough to protect both coasts against possible attack at the same time.

THE TUG OF WAR

EFFORTS TO DRAG AMERICA INTO EUROPEAN QUARRELS

CONGRESS

"The Tug of War," a 1939 political cartoon from the *Chicago Tribune,* pokes fun at Roosevelt as he tries to pull Congress out of its isolationist position and into European affairs.

THE AXIS MARCHES

While Congress was passing its neutrality laws, Germany, Italy, and Japan were planning to destroy all democracies. Benito Mussolini and his Italian Fascists looked for foreign conquest. Adolf Hitler came to power in Germany in 1933 with his Nazi Party. All Europe was filled with dread as Germany rearmed. The Nazis and Fascists formed the Axis alliance and counted on Japan for help.

In March 1938 Hitler seized Austria and made it part of greater Germany. Czechoslovakia was next. The Sudetenland part of it was mainly German already. By September 1938 Hitler's armies were ready to march. His harsh demands made compromise impossible. A general European war was about to start.

On September 26 Roosevelt cabled every nation a plea for peace. He sent Mussolini and Hitler desperate personal messages. But the Munich Agreement, signed by Germany, Britain, France, and Italy, gave the Sudetenland to Hitler. The American people began to realize that all the democracies were in fearful danger.

Hitler had promised to respect the independence of what was left of Czechoslovakia. In March 1939 he sent his armies smashing through the country. With Roosevelt's backing, Hull protested the "wanton lawlessness" of this "arbitrary force." Mussolini seized Albania. Roosevelt sent notes to the two dictators asking for pledges that they would attack no more. He wrote, "Heads of great governments in this hour are literally responsible for the fate of humanity in the coming years . . . history will hold them accountable for the lives and happiness of all." Nothing came of this but insulting evasion.

The European crisis mounted. Hitler demanded that Poland give Danzig to Germany and make concessions on the Polish Corridor. In August 1939 Germany and the Soviet Union reached an agreement that gave the Nazis a free hand. Roosevelt sent notes to the king of Italy, the president of Poland, and Hitler, pleading for peace. Hitler did not reply. He wanted a war of conquest. On September 1, 1939, he ordered his armies to attack Poland. France and Britain entered the fight. World War II had begun.

NEUTRALITY AND DEFENSE, 1939–41

For 27 months the United States was officially neutral. Actually it was on the side of Britain, France, and Poland from the start. Roosevelt summoned Congress to a special session while Hitler was overrunning Poland. It repealed the arms embargo on November 4, 1939. Shells, guns, and planes went to the British and French at once. Roosevelt rallied Latin America to united action.

The world was on fire. Congress voted $1.8 billion for defense. This was only a start. In April 1940 the Nazis seized Norway and Denmark. In May Hitler's armies entered the Netherlands and Belgium, swept over them, crushed French resistance, and forced the British to withdraw from Continental Europe. Roosevelt pointed out the horrible destruction of modern war to Congress on May 6, 1940. He said that no nation could be too strong and demanded means to stop any war maker "before he can establish strong bases within the territory of American vital interests." He asked for money for at least 50,000 planes and a much bigger Army and Navy. On May 31, as the Nazi sweep went on, he asked for another billion dollars.

Congress voted the money, and on July 5, 1940, voted another $5 billion. That summer the nation adopted a peacetime draft and began training a million men. With Canada, it set up a Joint Board of Defense. It gave hard-pressed Britain 50 destroyers. In return it got leases on Atlantic naval bases from Newfoundland to British Guiana.

Roosevelt called this the most momentous step in national defense since the Louisiana Purchase. In July 1940 a meeting in Havana of Latin American countries ended in complete agreement for the collective defense of the Americas.

This was the summer of a presidential campaign. Roosevelt was pitted against Wendell Willkie, the Republican candidate. Ordinarily the nation would not have elected a president to a third term. But to many people the crisis demanded an experienced leader. Willkie fought many of Roosevelt's domestic policies, but he refused to play politics with defense

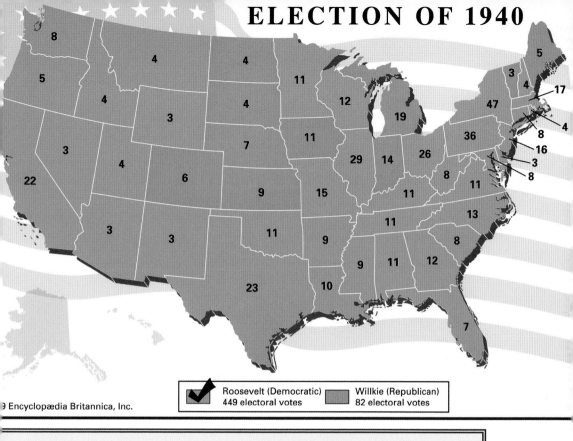

ELECTION OF 1940

✔ Roosevelt (Democratic) 449 electoral votes	Willkie (Republican) 82 electoral votes

9 Encyclopædia Britannica, Inc.

A map displays the electoral results of the U.S. presidential election of 1940. Roosevelt won 449 electoral votes to Wendell Willkie's 82.

measures. He boldly approved the destroyer deal and urged more help to Britain.

Willkie also accepted many New Deal reforms. He merely urged improved ways to carry them out. He was a leader of great vision and courage, but the nation refused to risk a change. Roosevelt won the election with 55 percent of the popular vote and 449 electoral votes to 82 for Willkie.

FREEDOM OF EXPRESSION OF RELIGION FROM WANT FROM FEAR

1791 1941

EVERYWHERE IN THE WORLD

JUNIOR MEMBERS ROUND TABLE. PENNSYLVANIA LIBRARY ASSOCIATION
PENNA ART W.P.A.

The Four Freedoms

Roosevelt saw the importance of moral preparation for war. In January 1941, in his State of the Union message, he told Congress that the United States looked forward "to a world founded upon four essential human freedoms." These were freedom of speech, freedom from want, freedom of worship, and freedom from fear. Roosevelt called for ensuring the latter through "a world-wide reduction of armaments to such a point and in such a thorough fashion that no nation will be in a position to commit an act of physical aggression against any neighbor—anywhere in the world."

A Works Progress Administration poster proclaims the Four Freedoms that were formulated by Roosevelt in his State of the Union speech on January 6, 1941.

ARSENAL OF DEMOCRACY

Six weeks after the election Roosevelt gave a radio talk warning the nation that if Britain were defeated, the Axis would rule the world and America would live at the point of a gun. "We must be the great arsenal of democracy," he said. He had one of his greatest measures in view—lend-lease.

The Lend-Lease Act became law on March 11, 1941, after a bitter Senate debate. It allowed the president to "sell, transfer title to, exchange, lease, lend, or otherwise dispose of" war materials to countries whose defense was vital to American security. These included weapons, machines, raw materials, and even repair services. The law permitted Allied nations to send warships to the United States for refitting and aircrews for training. It encouraged exchange of military information. It made the United States an active helper of all enemies of the Axis.

Congress voted $7 billion to support lend-lease. The money came just in time to help Britain and the Soviet Union, which

Hitler invaded in June 1941. Ships, planes, guns, and shells, along with food, clothing, and metals, steadily went overseas in both American and foreign ships. To protect delivery of lend-lease materials, American warships began patrolling North Atlantic sea lanes and American forces were stationed in Greenland and Iceland. After German submarines attacked American ships, the United States closed all German

Roosevelt and British Prime Minister Winston Churchill held meetings about war aims on warships off the coast of Newfoundland. On August 14, 1941, the two leaders issued their joint declaration, the Atlantic Charter.

consulates and ordered Atlantic patrol ships to shoot on sight.

In August 1941 Roosevelt met with British Prime Minister Winston Churchill aboard warships off the coast of Canada. After five days of talks they issued the Atlantic Charter. Although the United States was not yet officially in the war, this document outlined the Allies' war aims and called for the "final destruction of Nazi tyranny."

CHAPTER 7

Pearl Harbor and the United States at War

In the Pacific, events were leading to war. Japan was confident that Germany would defeat the Soviet Union and Britain. It wanted to complete the conquest of East Asia. In November 1941 Japan seized part of French Indochina and planted air bases in Thailand. It threatened Burma, the Dutch East Indies, and the Philippines.

The United States protested. A special Japanese group came to Washington

November 14 to begin discussions. They wanted the United States to accept Japanese conquests in Asia and do business as before. Secretary Hull refused. In return for full economic cooperation, he wanted Japan to leave Indochina and China. A complete deadlock was reached. On December 6 Roosevelt appealed directly to the Japanese emperor. The next day, Sunday, December 7, 1941, Japanese forces made a surprise attack on the U.S. naval base at Pearl Harbor in Hawaii. The United States was in World War II.

A U.S. battleship sinks during the surprise Japanese aerial attack on Pearl Harbor on December 7, 1941. Roosevelt asked Congress for a declaration of war on the following day.

A Declaration of War

On December 8, 1941, the day after Japan attacked Pearl Harbor, President Roosevelt went before Congress to ask for a declaration of war against Japan. In his message to Congress, he said:

Yesterday, December 7, 1941—a date which will live in infamy—the United States of America was suddenly and deliberately attacked by naval and air forces of the Empire of Japan. ...As commander in chief of the Army and Navy I have directed that all measures be taken for our defense. ...Hostilities exist. There is no blinking at the fact that our people, our territory, and our interests are in grave danger. With confidence in our armed forces—with the unbounded determination of our people—we will gain the inevitable triumph— so help us God. I ask that the Congress declare that since the unprovoked and dastardly attack by Japan on Sunday, December 7, a state of war has existed between the United States and the Japanese Empire.

On December 9 Roosevelt spoke to the nation by radio, describing the events that had led to war. The United States formally entered the war against Germany and Italy on December 11.

THE WAR EFFORT

"We are now in the midst of a war, not for conquest, not for vengeance, but for a world in which this nation, and all that this nation represents, will be safe for our children." So Roosevelt told the country in his war message of December 9, 1941. Congress passed

Americans threw themselves wholeheartedly into the war effort during World War II. Food, gasoline, and other goods were rationed. A poster by Jean Carlu promotes an all-out production effort in the defense plants.

the First and Second War Powers Acts and other laws to give him full authority. He had control over farming, manufacturing, labor, prices, wages, transportation, and allotment of raw materials. In turn he gave these powers to the right individuals, boards, or departments. Many war agencies were set up. Shifting and changing as needed, they brought nearly every activity of the country under government direction.

Early in 1942 Roosevelt called on industry to produce war equipment as it had never been produced before. He asked for 185,000 planes, 120,000 tanks, and 18 million deadweight tons of shipping—and he wanted it within two years. The Navy was to be built up into the greatest in the world, greater than all other navies combined. Eventually the armed forces would be expanded to a peak of about 14 million men and women. All Roosevelt's sons served in the armed forces. James was in the Marines, Elliott in the Army Air Force, and Franklin, Jr., and John in the Navy.

Helped by General George C. Marshall, chief of staff for the Army, and Admiral Ernest J. King, chief of staff for the Navy, Roosevelt worked out the main battle plans. With Winston Churchill, he set up the pattern of British-American unity. The

United States and Britain coordinated their war efforts through a Combined Chiefs of Staff.

National unity was more complete in World War II than in any war before. This was partly because Axis brutality deeply shocked and offended Americans. It was partly because Japan had treacherously attacked the United States. Then too people realized that the peace had not been kept after World War I. They wanted a lasting peace. On October 5, 1944, Roosevelt said, "We owe it to our posterity, we owe it to our heritage of freedom, we owe it to our God, to devote the rest of our lives and all our capabilities to the building of a solid, durable structure of world peace."

MARCH TO VICTORY

It was agreed early that the United States would fight hard on all fronts. Its main strength, however, would be used first to defeat Germany. For a year only a defensive war was fought in the Pacific. Some victories were won, however. In May 1942 a Japanese fleet was checked in the Battle of the Coral Sea. In June a larger Japanese force was defeated in the Battle of Midway.

In November the enemy took another severe beating off Guadalcanal.

The first heavy American blow at Germany was struck on November 8, 1942. A strong Anglo-American force landed in French North Africa and took the Nazi forces by surprise. The Americans and British, led by Lieutenant General Dwight D. Eisenhower, quickly took Algeria and invaded Tunis. Here they met a British army, under General Harold Alexander,

With their gun barrels covered against the spray of the sea, U.S. infantrymen gaze from their landing craft toward Omaha Beach on D-Day, June 6, 1944.

which had driven Erwin Rommel's troops out of Egypt and Tripoli. By May 12, 1943, the last German forces in Africa surrendered. The Allies now moved against *Festung Europa*—Fortress Europe.

The attack began on July 10, 1943. An amphibious assault was launched against Sicily. In 39 days American and British armies overran the island. The invasion of Italy followed on September 9. Naples was swiftly taken. A slugging battle was fought for Rome. It was finally taken in the spring of 1944. By then the major action had shifted to France, where the main German forces lay.

The world watched tensely. On June 6, 1944, Generals Eisenhower and Bernard Montgomery threw a huge army on the Normandy beaches. After a short but bitter fight, the beachheads were made secure. The port of Cherbourg fell on June 27. Then enough troops and material were assembled to enable the Anglo-American armies to break out of the beachheads and strike for Germany. On July 25 General Omar N. Bradley launched a great offensive, and the Germans were pushed back. By August 25 Paris was in Allied hands.

The advance into Germany went on with only one serious setback. The Battle of the Bulge, a Nazi counteroffensive of December

1944, temporarily threw American troops back, but it failed to hold them. Allied armies cleared the enemy from most of the area west of the Rhine River. The Soviets advanced from the east. The German armies were pounded by combined Allied blows. On May 7, 1945, the last Nazi forces surrendered to the Allies at Reims.

Meanwhile victory over Japan was well on the way. In 1943 American, Australian, and New Zealand forces took the offensive in the Pacific. The enemy was cleared out of most of New Guinea. The U.S. Navy captured Tarawa and two other islands in the Gilberts. Thereafter the United States, with more ships and planes than the enemy, was able to move much as it chose.

In July 1944 Saipan and Guam in the Marianas were taken. Both islands made good air bases. On October 20, American troops under General Douglas MacArthur landed on Leyte in the Philippines after a campaign of "island hopping" that began in Australia. By February 1945 they had captured Manila. Admiral William F. Halsey engaged the main Japanese naval force. The U.S. Navy destroyed most of the enemy fleet and virtually wiped out Japanese sea power.

CHAPTER 8

A New World Organization and a Fourth Term as President

R oosevelt directed the American war effort through close contact with Churchill and other British leaders. Later Joseph Stalin, premier of the Soviet Union, entered the conferences. Many Churchill-Roosevelt meetings were held in Washington. In August 1943 an Anglo-American Conference took place in Quebec. More Allied meetings were held later that year. First Roosevelt, Churchill, and Chiang Kai-shek of China met in Cairo. Then Roosevelt and Churchill went to Tehran for days of talks with Stalin. At the close they spoke of their hope for a "world family of democratic nations."

THE UNITED NATIONS CHARTER

Close to Roosevelt's heart was the formation of a new world organization, more effective than the old League of Nations. In this he had the help of Secretary Hull and of Congress. The Connolly and Fulbright resolutions, adopted by Congress in 1943, favored such a postwar organization. On May 30, 1944, the United States invited Britain, the Soviet Union, and China to a Washington conference to discuss world peace. Talks began August 21 at Dumbarton Oaks, a Washington mansion. A set of plans was submitted for study and comment by people of all nations.

In the summer and fall of 1944 another presidential campaign took place. The Democrats once more nominated Roosevelt. The Republicans chose Governor Thomas E. Dewey of New York. Both party platforms spoke vigorously for American participation in a world organization. Dewey, no less than

Roosevelt, was for the idea. Nearly the whole country was behind the move to organize peace and justice in a free world. In a radio broadcast on October 5, 1944, and in other speeches Roosevelt insisted that the United Nations be given power to keep peace by force and that American representatives be given authority to act quickly. No policeman could be useful, he said, if when he saw a burglar at work he had "to call a town meeting to issue a warrant before the felon could be arrested."

A map displays the electoral results of the U.S. presidential election of 1944. Roosevelt received 432 electoral votes to Thomas E. Dewey's 99.

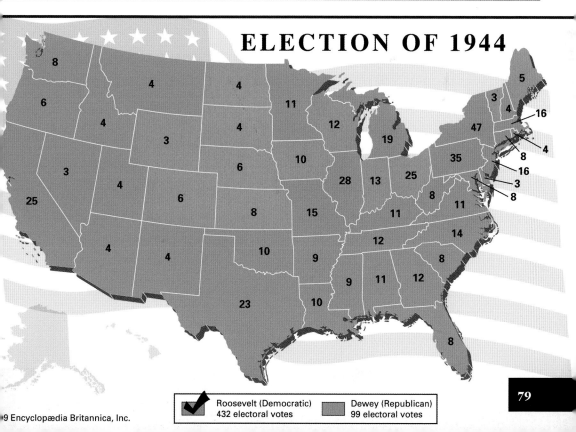

ELECTION OF 1944

Roosevelt (Democratic) 432 electoral votes	Dewey (Republican) 99 electoral votes	

Roosevelt was reelected for a fourth term. He won by a popular vote of 25,606,585 to Dewey's 22,014,745 and 432 electoral votes to 99. He clearly wanted the United Nations turned into a permanent peacetime group with full power to put down all war makers. In his 1945 message to Congress he said that the year just beginning "can be the greatest year of achievement in human history." It could see total victory over the Axis. "Most important of all, 1945 can and must see the substantial beginning of the organization of world peace. This organization must be the fulfillment of the promise for which men have fought and died in this war."

The next step was to hold a full international meeting and draw up a charter for the world organization. In February 1945, obviously in poor health and looking haggard, Roosevelt conferred with Churchill and Stalin at Yalta in Crimea. They discussed final war plans and peace questions.

A meeting was called at San Francisco for April 25, 1945, to turn the Dumbarton Oaks proposals into reality. Roosevelt planned to open the conference. The delegation he appointed to represent the United States was headed by Secretary of State E. R.

From left, British Prime Minister Winston Churchill, Roosevelt, and Soviet Premier Joseph Stalin pose with leading Allied officers at the Yalta Conference in February 1945. The leaders discussed the war's end and the structure of the postwar world.

Stettinius, Jr. Stettinius had succeeded Hull when the latter fell ill.

ROOSEVELT DIES

The delegates were gathering in San Francisco. American forces were thrusting deeper into Germany. Roosevelt went to Warm Springs, Georgia, for a short rest. On the morning of

Roosevelt's Burial

After his death, Roosevelt's body was taken by train from Warm Springs, Georgia, to Washington, D.C. From Union Station to the White House, the military procession passed streets filled with mourners. At the White House the casket was placed in the East Room, where the Roosevelt family held a private funeral service. In the evening the casket was carried by train to Hyde Park, New York. There the casket was put on a horse-drawn gun carriage and transported to the garden of Roosevelt's home, where he was buried.

Roosevelt's home is now a national historic site. The estate is also the site of the Franklin D. Roosevelt Presidential Library and Museum. Roosevelt dedicated the library, which was the first presidential library, in 1941.

April 12, 1945, he was busy signing documents and studying state papers. A painter was making sketches of him. Suddenly he slumped in his chair. He had suffered a cerebral hemorrhage. Death came swiftly. That evening Vice President Harry S. Truman was sworn in as president.

The wave of emotion that swept over much of the world was like that which followed Abraham Lincoln's death. Roosevelt's domestic measures had angered many people. Some of them disagreed violently with his foreign policies. But nearly everyone felt that the nation had lost a great leader. People had come to feel a warm regard for the man who had met the depression so bravely; who had carried through a broader and deeper set of reforms than any president before him; who had so ably led America in its greatest war effort; and who had played the principal part in starting the United Nations.

CONCLUSION

During his lifetime Franklin D. Roosevelt was at the same time one of the most loved and most hated men in American history. His supporters hailed him as the savior of his nation during the Great Depression and the defender of democracy during World War II. Opponents criticized him for undermining American free-market capitalism. They also blamed him for unconstitutionally expanding the

Statues of Roosevelt and his beloved dog, Fala, are seen in the Third Term room of the Franklin Delano Roosevelt Memorial in Washington, D.C. The memorial includes four outdoor "rooms," representing his four terms in office.

THEY (WHO) SEEK TO ESTABLISH SYSTEMS OF GOVERNMENT BASED ON THE REGIMENTATION OF ALL HUMAN BEINGS BY A HANDFUL OF INDIVIDUAL RULERS... CALL THIS A NEW ORDER. IT IS NOT NEW AND IT IS NOT ORDER.

powers of the federal government and for transforming the nation into a welfare state.

It is generally accepted by all, however, that Roosevelt was a brilliant politician, able to create a massive coalition of supporters that sustained the Democratic Party for decades after his death. There is also little argument that he was a talented administrator, able to retain leaders of diverse views within the executive branch. At his death most Americans were plunged into profound grief, testimony to the strong emotional attachment they felt for the man who had led them through two of the darkest periods in the nation's history. Although much of that emotion has disappeared over the years, Roosevelt's standing as one of the few truly great American presidents seems secure.

Glossary

alienate To cause someone to feel that he or she no longer belongs in a particular group, society, etc.

amphibious assault An attack carried out by land, sea, and air forces acting together.

appropriation Money set aside for a specific use.

bankruptcy A condition of financial failure caused by not having the money to pay debts.

country squire A well-to-do country resident or owner of a country estate.

electoral vote A vote in the electoral college, the system by which the president and vice president of the United States are elected.

foreclose To take legal measure to end a mortgage and take possession of the mortgaged property because the conditions of the mortgage have not been met.

Great Depression Severe economic downturn that began in 1929 and lasted until about 1940. Although it started in the United States, it caused drastic declines in production and severe unemployment in almost every country of the world.

intellect The capacity for knowledge.

landslide An overwhelming victory in a political election.

mortgage A legal agreement in which a person borrows money to buy property (such as a house) and pays back the money over a period of years.

Nazi Party A political party that came to power in Germany in 1933 under the leadership of Adolf Hitler. It governed by totalitarian methods until the collapse of the Nazi regime in 1945 at the end of World War II.

party platform A declaration of principles and policies adopted by a political party.

poliomyelitis An infectious viral disease of the nervous system that usually begins with general symptoms such as fever, headache, nausea, fatigue, and muscle pains and spasms and is sometimes followed by a more-serious and permanent paralysis of muscles in one or more limbs, the throat, or the chest; also called polio.

public service Government employment.

quarantine To isolate.

stock market A system or place where shares of various companies are bought and sold. The shares are called stock.

sustain To provide what is needed for something or someone to exist or continue.

Tammany Hall The corrupt Democratic organization that dominated New York City politics in the 19th and early 20th centuries.

tariff A tax on products coming into or leaving a country.

typhoid fever An infectious disease marked by fever, diarrhea, fatigue, headache, and intestinal inflammation.

undermine To weaken or ruin secretly or gradually.

vigorous Done with force and energy.

welfare state A system in which the government undertakes to offer programs to protect citizens against economic risks and uncertainties at some, or all, stages of their lives.

For More Information

Franklin D. Roosevelt Four Freedoms Park
1 FDR Four Freedoms Park
Roosevelt Island, NY 10044
(212) 204-8831
Website: http://www.fdrfourfreedomspark
.org
Four Freedoms Park, a public space located
on the southern tip of Roosevelt Island
in New York City, honors the life and
legacy of President Roosevelt through its
educational programs.

Franklin D. Roosevelt Presidential Library
and Museum
National Archives
4079 Albany Post Road
Hyde Park, NY 12538
(845) 486-7770
Website: http://www.fdrlibrary.marist.edu

The FDR Presidential Library and Museum was constructed under President Roosevelt's direction and was opened for visits and research in 1941. The museum collection includes a great variety of items related to the public and private lives of Franklin and Eleanor Roosevelt, including his collections of stamps, coins, naval art, and ship models as well as furniture, clothing, and personal items. The archives holds family papers, manuscripts, and historical photographs and sound and motion picture recordings.

The Library of Congress
101 Independence Avenue SE
Washington, DC 20540
(202) 707-5000
Website: http://www.loc.gov
The Library of Congress is the world's largest library and the national library of the United States. Its collections include more than 160 million books, recordings, photographs, maps, and manuscripts. Its website includes information on the Great Depression and World War II (http://www.loc.gov/teachers /classroommaterials /presentationsandactivities

/presentations/timeline/depwwii)
as well as links to topics on the reaction
of Americans to the Great Depression,
the Dust Bowl, Franklin D. Roosevelt
and the New Deal, and race relations in
the 1930s and 1940s.

Miller Center
P.O. Box 400406
Charlottesville, VA 22904
(434) 924-7236
Website: http://millercenter.org /president
/fdroosevelt
The Miller Center, based at the University
of Virginia, is a nonpartisan research
facility focused on the history of the U.S.
presidency. Its Franklin D. Roosevelt
page provides a biography and transcripts
of key speeches.

The National WWII Museum
945 Magazine Street
New Orleans, LA 70130
(504) 528-1944
Website: http://www.nationalww2museum.org
This museum provides an in-depth explo-
ration of the U.S. role in World War II
through artifacts, multimedia exhibits,
and first-person oral histories.

Roosevelt Campobello International Park
459 Route 774
Welshpool, New Brunswick E5E 1A4
Canada
(877) 851-6663
Website: http://www.fdr.net
Located on Campobello Island, New
      Brunswick, this park is the site of
      Franklin D. Roosevelt's summer cottage,
      where the president and his family spent
      summer vacations.

WEBSITES

Because of the changing nature of Internet
links, Rosen Publishing has developed an
online list of websites related to the subject
of this book. This site is updated regularly.
Please use this link to access the list:

http://www.rosenlinks.com/PPPL/frank

For Further Reading

Brennan, Linda Crotta. *Franklin D. Roosevelt's Presidency* (Presidential Powerhouses). Minneapolis, MN: Lerner Publications, 2015.

Darman, Peter. *The Allied Invasion of Europe* (World War II). New York, NY: Rosen Publishing, 2013.

Darman, Peter. *Attack on Pearl Harbor: America Enters World War II* (World War II). New York, NY: Rosen Publishing, 2013.

Duignan, Brian, ed. *The Great Depression* (Economics: Taking the Mystery Out of Money). New York, NY: Britannica Educational Publishing and Rosen Educational Services, 2013.

Duncan, Dayton, and Ken Burns. *The Dust Bowl: An Illustrated History.* San Francisco, CA: Chronicle Books, 2012.

Egan, Timothy. *The Worst Hard Time: The Untold Story of Those Who Survived the Great American Dust Bowl.* Boston, MA: Houghton Mifflin Company, 2013.

Ellis, Catherine, ed. *Key Figures of World War II* (Biographies of War). New York, NY: Britannica Educational Publishing and Rosen Educational Services, 2016.

Evans, A.A., and David Gibbons. *The Illustrated Timeline of World War II* (History Timelines). New York, NY: Rosen Publishing, 2012.

Freedman, Russell. *Eleanor Roosevelt: A Life of Discovery.* N.p.: Paw Prints, 2008.

Hosch, William L., ed. *World War II: People, Politics, and Power* (America at War). New York, NY: Britannica Educational Publishing and Rosen Educational Services, 2010.

Kesselring, Mari. *How to Analyze the Works of Franklin D. Roosevelt* (Essential Critiques). Minneapolis, MN: ABDO Publishing Company, 2013.

Leuchtenburg, William Edward. *Franklin D. Roosevelt and the New Deal, 1932–1940.* New York, NY: Harper Perennial, 2009.

Marrin, Albert. *FDR and the American Crisis.* New York, NY: Alfred A. Knopf, 2015.

Pasachoff, Naomi. *Frances Perkins: Champion of the New Deal* (Oxford Portraits). New York, NY: Oxford University Press, 1999.

Wallenfeldt, Jeff, ed. *A New World Power: America from 1920 to 1945* (Documenting America: The Primary Source Documents of a Nation). New York, NY: Britannica Educational Publishing and Rosen Educational Services, 2013.

Williamson, David G. *The Cold War.* London, UK: Hodder Education, 2013.

Index